Devil in a Coma

Mark Lanegan

**WHITE
RABBIT**

First published in Great Britain in 2021 by White Rabbit,
an imprint of The Orion Publishing Group Ltd
Carmelite House, 50 Victoria Embankment
London EC4Y 0DZ

An Hachette UK Company

1 3 5 7 9 10 8 6 4 2

A CIP catalogue record for this book is
available from the British Library.

ISBN (Hardback) 978 1 3996 0184 9
ISBN (eBook) 978 1 3996 0185 6
ISBN (Audio) 978 1 3996 0186 3

Printed and bound in Great Britain by Clays Ltd, Elcograf, S.p.A

www.whiterabbitbooks.co.uk
www.orionbooks.co.uk

Devil in a Coma

Also by Mark Lanegan

Don't wake me, I'm sleeping

Foreword

Idle hands are the devil's workshop. Mark could not even be hindered by near death. The way I saw it, he bailed on America for literal greener pastures as a survival technique – mentally, physically and spiritually, and presumably with the luck of the Irish. An existential global crisis was emerging with the advent of the COVID-19 pandemic and little did any of us know you couldn't escape it.

Mark is a prolific fellow. And anyone who understands artists knows that this attribute comes at a cost. '*Devil in a Coma* is a memoir of the Covid experience that goes off the rails several times into other shit' – those are his words.

FOREWORD

He is a fighter and death came knocking. Imagine: the Kerry countryside backdrop with an internal hell emerging. Needless to say, he caught the wretched thing. A three-month journey with a third of it being spent unconscious. The havoc — a sucker punch to your being, oxygen, blood, failure, panic, insomnia, hallucinations, delusions, how real the dream is, tripping on a sick astral plane in the nether. This virus is also a disease of the brain which, if overactive, will naturally send you to far-off places, all while taking your breath away. It attacks tenfold. He was intubated, deaf, alone, and slipping away. There were end-of-life talks, a potential tracheotomy for one of the greatest voices of all time ... a universal cruelty. A recollection that is factual, fragmented, cursed and triumphant, and whose revival enriches the soul.

Wesley Eisold

Devil in a Coma

Deaf / Apples from a Tree

I had been feeling weak and sick for a few days
and then woke up one morning completely deaf.
My equilibrium shaky, and my mind in a sur-
real psychedelic dream-state, I lost my footing at
the top of the stairs. Head over heels over head,
I knocked myself out on the windowsill as I
crashed down the narrow staircase at my house.
Bang. My wife was out horseback riding for the
day, and I came to hours later still unable to hear
a thing, unable to move, two huge opened welts
on my head, and my knee not supporting any
weight.

For two days I tried to get from stairwell to
couch, with no success. I could not move, nor
could my wife support my two-hundred-pound
body, so I lay suffering on some blankets on the

hard floor for forty-eight hours. My ribs were cracked, my spine bruised, battered and sore, and my already chronically messed-up knee gone again, as if some tendons were ripped or a ligament severed. My leg was useless. Every attempted breath was a battle, no matter how hard I tried to take a natural one. Though I refused to go to hospital my wife finally called an ambulance behind my back and I was wheeled out of my yard on a gurney. I eventually ended up in intensive care, unable to draw oxygen, and was diagnosed with some exotic new strain of the coronavirus for which there was no cure, of course. I was put into a medically induced coma, none of which I remembered.

Six weeks later and still in the ICU, three-thirty a.m., wide-ass awake now, raw as fuck, still fighting for air. Wiped out from severe insomnia and the twin kicks to the nuts that were the virus and my injuries, I started wishing I were still in my medical blackout. It was beyond evident that as much as I craved some temporary oblivion, the woefully inadequate amounts of Seroquel, Xanax and OxyContin I was being given were not going to put me down for more than a few minutes at a time – probably since I'd been self-administering elephant-sized doses of the same shit on and off for years. I was a specialist at finding the doctors that would willingly write scripts for nearly anything I wanted, working psychiatric clinics, urgent care facilities and your average general practitioners and dentists. In California you couldn't throw a rock without hitting a medical facility. At the same time I cultivated a large circle of shady Craigslist amateur pharmacists who filled in the days between my legal doses with bottles of black market pills. To me it was second nature to eat tablets like candy and I'd been doing it so long I'd forgotten what they actually *felt* like unless I was caught without for a time and then started again. And, of course, it never occurred to me that there might come a time when I would legitimately need some. The myopia that largely dogged me my entire life kept me rooted in the here and now, and hardly anything else ever crossed my mind, especially if it was to take place in some far-off distant future never-never land. Such places did not exist in my limited scope of reality.

The older dude, Dennis, one of my three roommates, groaned and rolled around, tugging uncomfortably on his IV. Nobody was happy here, I could tell you that much. I was intubated, a breathing tube down my throat, for the first full three weeks after being dumped at the hospital by the ambulance workers that had rolled my damaged body on a stretcher through my front garden. They had put me in the back of the vehicle where I wheezed and fought to take a proper breath of air to no avail.

Now, a month later, having been visited by nothing but bizarre dreams, strange visions, shadowy darkness, untrustworthy memories and recurring hallucinations, all hallmarks of near-death experiences, I was conscious again. Still in intensive care, catheter shoved up my dick, every attempt at taking a deep breath – even a yawn – met with the unwelcome sensation of being slammed in the chest with a twenty-pound sledgehammer. Apparently my light had almost gone out permanently more than once, according to the doctors and nurses. I was asked three times a day if I knew where I was and rarely gave a correct answer. Sometimes I felt as though I were pulling steel high up on the skeleton of a stage, taking down one long, round, metal ceiling pole while standing on an identical one twenty feet off the ground. Or I'd be driving miles to deliver drugs to someone in another city, or dismantling a stolen car after midnight for parts to sell or trade. Sometimes I'd be boxing potatoes and stacking them on pallets in the spud factory or using metal hooks to buck hay bales onto a tractor under the intense eastern Washington summer sun, or I'd be drunkenly cooking pancake and egg breakfasts in a busy restaurant after drinking and carousing all night; a few of the activities among many I had participated in in my youth. At times I felt I were on a tour bus in the States or the UK, and I remember thinking I was on a train, travelling through Australia for a while. China, the Middle East, the plains of Canada, and where I had grown up in the Pacific Northwest were all places I imagined I was holding court amongst the damned. I had no idea where these delusions came from but they were ever-present.

I was slightly aware as I came to that I was hooked up to medical equipment, but it felt as though the rooms where I lay were always radically different, always changing. A house, a backstage somewhere, etc., and while the rooms were forever different, the view out the window was always the same. In reality I was in hospital twenty minutes from my home in County Kerry, Ireland, and I didn't realise the view in my dream was the sight out of the window in the hospital room.

One night I dreamt I was living in a large, windowless basement apartment off a rain-wet main drag in Seattle with several of my ex-girlfriends and ex-wives, many of whom detested me in real life, all in harmony with each other, and I felt a peace come over me. Another night I dreamt I was back at my former home in California, a place I always swore I'd never leave, magically flying above the fruit trees with my beloved little dog in my arms, pulling fragrant apples off the treetops and feeding them to him as he licked my face just as he had the day he died and broke my heart. I woke up from that one crying, with my shirt soaked in tears of despair.

€€€€€€€€€€€€€€€€€€€€€€€€€€€€€€€

&&&&&&&&&&&&&&&&&&&&&&&&&&

On the Bridge

Stood on the
                bridge stammering stuttering
    shivering
teeth jackhammering
wind chill
barbiturates, sorrow

and grief

Despair will kick your door in
And rip your fucking heart out

It would be so easy to
                let go of this
reality
if there were another one
                somewhere in sight
a stronger one

corrosive like battery acid

something to burn

this dream

        right outta my

head

Fuck All / Hillbilly Nostradamus

After almost two months it seemed like I had been in hospital forever. With no discernible light in the tunnel, patience level below zero, I was at a crossroad where I would have gladly stepped in front of a train just to change the outcome of the day, every dark hour slowly running into the next. I had suffered through so many self-imposed hard times in the past but this was beyond the pale. With people all over the world being hospitalised and dying on a daily basis, and since there appeared to be sweet fuck all anyone could do for you, what was the actual point in going through this medical reacharound? You either caught it or didn't, got sick or stayed well, slowly survived it, or were laid low and died – and my personal experience so far seemed to bear out this hypothesis. Now that I was back in the world, and knew the score, it felt as if my days consisted only of the occasional blood pressure check, a plate of food I never ate, and extreme boredom, pain and unhappiness. My fellow patients were all much older than me and many whimpered and sobbed constantly. The happier ones loved to talk nonstop. I wore a pair of headphones round the clock so as not to be drawn into conversation.

As I started to slowly regain my shattered wits, the deal I'd made with a night-time doctor for extra pharmaceuticals was predictably fucked, and I neither received the meds I'd been promised nor was I given the freedom to have a smoke at the window before lights out. Everything felt like something that was happening again, an unwelcome déjà vu, with the end result preordained. The hillbilly Nostradamus in me had often been mythically correct as to a handful of likely outcomes in any given situation, but what my self-destructive mind was telling me here was nothing I wanted to entertain. Still, I found it impossible to keep these unwanted thoughts from invading my head fifty times a day. I was so angry at being deprived of the cigarette I'd been promised, I stopped interacting with staff for a good week or so. This was unnecessary torture. My arms were covered in nicotine patches since a smoke was not gonna happen. If I were mercifully able to drift off for fifteen minutes, my mind would always replay the same vision, in which I was walking alone on the wintertime roadside, scanning the parcels of fields behind ancient rock walls, under black skies, looking for relief that didn't exist. I knew friends and associates from the past would likely assume this latest spectacular deep dive were drug-related, but I was a million miles away from giving a damn about that, couldn't give a fuck what anybody thought.

Nobody had ever honestly believed I was clean the fifteen years I was, anyway. My father, a heavy drinker well into his seventies, had called me at four o'clock one afternoon from his home in Alaska, drunk, while I was washing my clothes at a laundromat in Pasadena. He began to accuse me of being on drugs which at five years clean pissed me off. I called him the next day when I knew he'd be sober and politely asked that he not phone me while he was drinking. He didn't call me again for nearly twenty years.

From the moment I was brought out of my chemically induced sleep and was told what had happened and where I had been, I was determined to survive this nightmare, even though I had very little say, actually, *no* say in the matter, and had zero ammo to fight with.

And I was totally and fully debilitated. More and more this was reminiscent of an unending stretch in county jail that I couldn't shake, with my trial date being intentionally undetermined, constantly moved around just to keep me inside. It felt like the longer I was kept here the worse I got, not the other way around. After all I was less than minutes from my place, but my leg, back, lungs and psyche were still so twisted up I could hardly even get around with a walker. I found the situation to be intolerably fucked. Time dragged insidiously on . . .

I had been brought in on Saint Paddy's Day and now it was May ninth. Three months . . . this was fucking ludicrous. I tried my best to suppress sneezing or coughing because every time I did, my entire upper body was wracked with sharp spasms of pain and severe discomfort. Whatever was in this shitwagon I'd caught a ride on, it was no fucking joke. I'd taken my share of well-deserved asskickings over the years but this thing was trying to dismantle me, body and mind, and I could see no end to it in sight.

Five thirty a.m., lights flashing on and off, nurses already laughing and starting to work across the hallway; I couldn't have slept five minutes if I wanted to, and I wanted to very fucking much, thank you. I had to get out of here, that was paramount. One of the charming side effects of the Covid was the loss of smell and taste, rendering everything I tried to eat seem like it had been cooked up in a cat box. The more the doctors kept stressing the importance of eating and endlessly pushing the food on me, the less likely I was to put any of it in my mouth, and after another tortuous attempted blood-taking session, I flat out refused to be a human pincushion anymore, causing a stand-off I wasn't going to lose as long as I were conscious. My kidneys reportedly were blown out, and while I was in the coma I had been on dialysis, with the doctors daily predicting doom and gloom, prepping my wife and immediate circle of friends for my imminent undoing, lifetime dialysis or transplant. They told my wife I held the record for the longest stay in this condition to survive at this institution.

The nurses were a saving grace, very kind and caring, and I was amazed at their warmth towards all the patients, even the openly unhappy and borderline unfriendly ones such as myself. I became pals with a man named Francie who worked as a porter at the hospital, and he was there every day offering support, bringing chocolate and sausage rolls, the only things I could stomach besides milk.

I knew where my remaining veins were hiding

and could have accessed them if allowed, but the last thing a doctor wants is for a patient to do something they can't. They tried to make a deal with me: let them try to extract from an artery once or try five times to find a conventional vein. I immediately vetoed this plan. I'd be goddamned before I let an actual doctor or anyone else stick me in an artery, a painful mess of an affair. I had accidentally shot heroin into one before and the memory of that wretched experience I had never forgotten. And five more tries at hitting a normal vein was not going to work for me, either. I asked them to please hit my jugular and be done with it but the young physician expressed trepidation at that, never having taken blood from someone's neck before.

Love story

Don't love anything too much
because a vein will open
it'll pour out a river
when you're already drowning

Close the book if the story's over
cash out at curtain call
This is clearly the fall
I won't get up from

Predestination Concepts /
Self-fulfilling Prophecy

Predestination concept
self-fulfilling prophecies
and all that

You gotta be prepared for the worst case
scenario but you don't wanna dwell on it
either

Some guys implode under the pressure of
    possible impending ruin
some crawl into a bottle
or a spoon
but you don't wanna crawl too far in
or that can be the disaster itself

It's absolutely possible to will the impossible
    to life and
when someone does something habitually,
    they're bound
to slack off a bit over time
and make mistakes which might put them in
    danger

You have to be vigilant if you're gonna
    survive

You gotta sleep with
one eye open

Yesterday and Tomorrow

In the back of my mind I had always known those remaining veins were gonna prove valuable at some point. For fifteen years I avoided giving blood for two reasons: first, I jealously guarded what was left in case of an emergency, in case I came to a place someday with my back against a wall, where only a shot of something strong was going to get me through. And second, to find a vein in the first place was just so fucking unpleasant. I hadn't used an outfit in years, but if I were to be diagnosed with some terminal illness, you could bet the farm I would then. Due to my past addiction, for years my life had been an endless search for a place to bury a needle, but like everything else I ever cared about, I maniacally burned through them all like there was no tomorrow until suddenly it was tomorrow, with me standing dick in hand thinking it was still yesterday.

Torch Song

Five thousand miles
harvested in bone orchard
Día de los Muertos
Agony, death letter, repeat
Sodium glare and
panic room
sex bible
of salt-mine escapee
Here come the jingle-jangle
patchwork man
sewn up

to put a bullet

through a paper donkey

¥$£¥$£¥$£¥$£¥$£¥$£¥$$¥$!

Rise and Shine

I woke up to the smell of shit as a porter cleaned the excrement off the ass and back of the patient in the next bed over. Not the most pleasant way to wake up, but good morning! I'd stopped eating altogether and ironically milk was the only thing I could get down. Milk, something I had found disgusting my entire life, and now it was my lifeblood. Every day a cadre of doctors and nurses tried to convince me to let them draw blood which of course I wasn't gonna do unless I was the one drawing. As they tried to cajole me

I stonewalled and looked through them with the dead eyes of a shark until they gave up and left me alone. Luckily Francie was always around and they also let my wife come and go as she wished, so I had two important allies. Every day my wife Shelley showed up with a list of friends and family who were sending their love. On the one hand it was nice to hear, but on the other it depressed me, having everyone knowing my business.

If I wanted you to know

I'd have told you myself, right?
Rumour and innuendo
shit talking and gossip
are for the motherfucking birds
even though I've been guilty of such on rare
   occasion

keep my business under yr hat please
and let me keep my own shit
to myself

Wounded / Death Report

A nurse told me they were going to move me into his room, a very large one. He said the change in scenery would do me good so I went for it. That was a mistake. In my previous room I was at least fifteen years younger than anybody else but this new room was basically filled with living corpses in their eighties and nineties. Great change of scenery. My first morning there I opened my eyes to find an old lady rummaging through my things and taking my chocolate, eating some as she went about her thievery. I supposed when you got so close to the end everything was in play, as she obviously didn't give a damn, so I reached past her into my stash and gave her all the chocolate I had.

I would turn my phone on once daily just to see how many Covid deaths had taken place world-wide the previous day. My resolve was starting to fade and my dreams started to become more sinister. I dreamt my mother emptied a card-board box full of large wolf spiders on me and as I frantically brushed them off my face she stood laughing and said, 'This is what you have com-ing you selfish prick.' Being on the receiving end of her continual curses was old hat but it made me angry as hell that I couldn't even die without being insulted by her.

Meanwhile I was losing weight at an incred-ible speed. I was at least twenty-five pounds lighter now than when I had arrived. Two doc-tors sat down to tell me how dangerously close to the edge I was and how I'd better start eating and let them take blood to check the state of my kidneys. I agreed to give them a urine sample instead, and when they found blood and proteins in it indicating kidney damage I honestly did not give a shit because at this point I would just as soon let the chips fall where they might rather than endure any more of what felt like a steady regime of mind-bending torture and ridiculous ennui.

A night-time nurse caught me taking a drag off a smoke at four in the morning and raised so much hell that had I two healthy legs I'd have been inclined to try and beat him down, but I couldn't have hurt a child, the state I was in.

'I'm reporting you to the doctor,' he said.

'Go ahead you son of a bitch' was my response.

Other than the odd occurrence such as that, I mainly didn't say a word all day. After all, I had not asked anyone to bring me here, nor had anyone asked if I wanted to be there. It tasted like a jail cocktail with a viral chaser. As far as I could tell, nothing was really being done to heal me, it was all so much bullshit and the daily death reports convinced me that this was just a waiting room at the morgue, that at some time in the near future my number was gonna come up and I would be another casualty in this sterile and uninviting place. I began to have fantasies in which I walked to the centre of a huge field surrounded by forest with trees a mile high, emptied several cans of petrol everywhere, threw a lit Zippo into the grass and then stood in the middle of it waiting to be immolated. And I was so very tired. Constant daydreams of leaving pervasive, I couldn't shake this shadow hanging over my head, nor could I shut it off, even on the rare occasions I slept.

One night I wheeled my walker to the window and spent a very long time contemplating whether or not a fall from four storeys would do the job of finishing me, all of my godlike delusions disappeared. My thoughts were consumed by the memories of nonstop intentional and un-intentional damage I had caused my entire life and the darkness I had willingly invited in. I'd lived like a fire raging through a skyscraper, a cauldron of negative energy. When I would think about the multitude of dead and broken romances, lies, dishonest promises and false hopes of past situations and relationships, my ruthlessness, thieving and using, missed opportunities and heartache would nearly make me choke back tears. And I might have cried had self-pity been in my playbook, but I was acutely aware that I had asked for this and had it coming, like every other painful event in my life. I held the real stains brought on from this sickness inside, they were the wounds no one but myself was ever going to see, not even my long-suffering wife Shelley who had largely stuck with me through years of my destructive behaviour, deception, barely contained violent impulses and bullshit promises to change for the better. She had tested positive for Covid when I'd been hospitalised, but never developed any symptoms. After years of being correctly identified as the deviant bad actor I was, I'd finally happened upon one who believed against her better judgement that I was a misunderstood poet with something worthwhile to give the world. But that book had been closed forever long ago and all salvation was so far away it was out of sight.

I had stumbled through the darkness for so long that daylight was blinding. And when I was left to my own devices, I would generally go on a self-destructive tear. Shelley showed up on more than one occasion just in time to bring me back from the edge, saving me at the expense of her own well-being, sending her into the deep blues herself. This brought on a temporary guilt, but I was constitutionally incapable of really thinking about anyone but myself and would start scheming my next self-serving move before I could think too much about any pain I'd wrought. This was my pay-back, plain and simple.

Miss Me

Do you think that you might miss me?
Slowly goes the night
afraid that you might miss me
afraid that you could love
and lose
so slowly turns the clock

I Dreamt of the Rising Tide

In late April 2021 I made up my mind to leave the hospital; the constant noise, lights and sleeplessness were doing a number on my head and I could feel I was on the edge of an explosion. A time bomb out of time, drowning in the misery of my fellow patients, and as someone who preferred his own company, I found this scene excruciating. When the porter brought breakfast around I declined as usual, told her I wanted to leave that day and asked that she help facilitate that. Four hours later a doctor came by and began trying to talk me into staying, a conversation which lasted three hours.

'You are still very ill and the hospital is the safest place for you.'

'Until when?' I asked.

'You have a very long road ahead of you to recovery. Besides having Covid, you have multiple other injuries that are not going to heal overnight. I can't give you a specific date but it's going to take quite a while.'

This was extremely unwelcome news. As usual I had obviously misjudged the severity of the situation. I decided to give it a little more time until I had formed a more solid plan.

That night I had an extremely vivid dream. I was on a beach at dusk, standing at the water's edge when the tide started coming in with a vengeance, and I watched as a boat approaching the shore suddenly caught fire and sank before my eyes. As I turned around to leave I could see that between myself and the woods behind were what looked like thousands of snakes coiled together blocking my path. Every time I wanted out something was in my way . . .

Trapped

I found an old rusty metal trap
out by the old canal
near my childhood home

I cleaned it up and set it back

in the muddy banks

hoping to catch a muskrat

just for the rotten fuck of it

On my way home through the fields

I came across a cow stuck in the mud

a huge animal in distress

I tried for hours to push it free

but I was just a boy, not a tractor

Exhausted and nearing nightfall

I walked back to the canal

set off the trap with a stick

and threw it in the water

Months later I trudged back that same way

and found the intact skeleton of the cow

I'd tried to set free

This Might Sting a Little

My great-great-great-grandfather Thomas Lanigan was born in 1794 in Kilkenny, Ireland, and at age thirty migrated to Nova Scotia. From there my family spread out across North America, mainly the Canadian Maritimes. Some ended up on Prince Edward Island, some in New Brunswick, my great-grandmother landing there from the Scottish Highlands. My great-grandfather Alexander came down from Canada to Wisconsin, where his wife gave birth to a son, my grandfather William. William settled in South Dakota and fought for the United States in the trenches of France in World War One, surviving and making a home out west in Washington state, where he worked in the shipyards during World War Two and had my father when he was an older man. My maternal grandmother was born in Wales to Welsh parents and my maternal grandfather, who was shot to death on his front lawn before I was born, I knew nothing about – being largely estranged from that side of my family, I had never received any more information than that. All I knew is that the seemingly brash intensity of my ancestors' behaviour made it nearly a miracle that I had come out of that fucked-up fray.

Hospitals and institutions, those were two places I knew intimately, though. When I was barely out of my teens I already had so many long hospital stays that my impatience level went through the roof if I ever ended up in one. Jails, rehabs and psych wards were also familiar places to be avoided in my book; when I was twelve my own mother tried to 5150 me but my father stepped in knowing she just wanted to see me gone, punished and locked up out of her sight no matter the cost. On one occasion around that same time I was standing at the window of my basement bedroom listening to music when my mother burst into the room. Dragging the stylus across my record, and breaking the record in half, she yelled at me maniacally then turned around and slammed my door on her way out. I had a buck knife in my hand and as soon as she left I threw it against the door, where it stuck in the wood. Seconds later she was back, saw the knife in the door and went hysterical, screaming that I had tried to kill her. This incident set off a war between my father and her, and when she refused to get a grip on herself he held her against the wall and ripped the phone cord out of the wall to prevent her from calling the police to report me for attempted murder.

Nearly every dispute, drama or argument in our unhappy household placed me squarely in the middle of it. These were weekly occurrences at least, often daily. Straight out of the box, I learned to avoid her at all costs if possible, and I left my childhood behind very early on without a single happy memory of myself and her. Her bitter dislike of me was so obvious I would often be doing nothing at all and come under attack anyway. The one and only time I made her authentically laugh was when her own mother were staying with us and I yelled *fuck you* at her when she tried to tell me I couldn't leave the house.

I took direction from my father, the only voice of reason in our home, although he was often absent, living a second life elsewhere to escape the savage war constantly fought at our house. My place in our family tree was the lowest hanging, most easily pounded piñata, the anti-protagonist, always living under the threat of taking a mental or physical beatdown from this sick person and always fighting back with feral intensity. I didn't know why I was the constant target, but neither did I ever care, protecting myself was my main concern and every dread-filled moment I was alone in her presence set me on high alert. She tried so many times and so many ways to destroy me, I would have murdered her if I ever had the opportunity. After searching my room and finding a weed pipe, she gave an ultimatum: either I see a psychologist or she would turn me in to the police, her favourite ultimate go-to threat, one she had made good on before. Of course I chose the psych doctor, who after talking with me for ten minutes said, 'I think it's your mother who needs help, not you.' Had it not been for my father, things could have gone very dark on me, and when they finally divorced I was happier than I'd ever been.

My long rap sheet of juvenile crimes, however, landed my ass in serious trouble as soon as I turned eighteen, and had it not been for the fact that nearly every charge and arrest was drug- and alcohol-related (meaning the judge siphoned me off to a treatment program as opposed to the prison sentence I'd been handed down), my life could have been even darker. My mother quit her job as a college lecturer on early childhood education and went to work at the Hanford nuclear plant, and when the FBI visited my father's house to question him about his take on her mental health, I held back my laughter at his honest and humorous answers to the questions. It was obvious he was having fun. Not one to stab anyone in the back, he brought smiles from the government agents with his brief answers that screamed *watch out, buyer beware.*

My first stepfather was a hellraising biker covered in homemade tattoos. We would go hunting together for rabbits to eat but he would also sometimes attach a scope to his rifle and blow away birds for sport at such a distance there was no retrieving their bodies. He was *that* kind of guy.

My second stepfather was a sick right-wing fanatic in his nineties who watched Fox News round the clock and gave my nephew some right-wing literature for his fifteenth birthday. He was *that* kind of guy.

The only man in my life I ever truly respected was my own father, who sadly had not the best luck in the marriage game himself.

Father and Son

I carried an axe into the woods
twice a day in summertime
with my father to split the logs
he would cut with his chainsaw
a massacre of trees

He could be a strict taskmaster
and we went about our work with me in
    sullen angry silence

That was the only time we were in conflict
because at heart he shunned conflict
he just wanted to get by quietly
had enough of war
but on those occasions he wanted
his son to work a war began
because his son was at heart
something different, half-father
but part-spider too
part-snake and part-hateful fiend
part-wolf caught in a trap
thirsty for blood and revenge and chaos and
　　escape
digging graves and brooding discontent

As a boy one of my many obsessions
was getting to France somehow
to join the Foreign Legion

Now I've been to France
many times in fact but I never joined

an army, instead I fought an imaginary war
my entire life and was the only casualty
dying over and over in countless ways
always by my own hand

If I were able to see my father again
I would tell him that I am just like him now
that I shun conflict and have had enough
of war and that I would be happy to go into
the woods twice a day with him
to split logs

Four Angels

Determined to get some quality sleep one night,
I saved up my Seroquel and Xanax until I had
a pretty good stash I was sure would put me
down. I fell into a slumber quickly and found
myself wandering in a bombed-out tenement.

As I entered the first floor a giant being with a helmet on and wings flat against his back turned and stared at me with the most magnetic blue eyes.

'What are you doing here boy?' he asked.

'I'm trying to find a way out, I feel like I'm dying here.'

'You're not dying, you are just suffering. Hang on and you'll make it out, don't worry.'

I heard a noise and turned around to see two more of these beings, and as they conversed, a very large fourth joined the room, this one obviously in charge.

'Go back, kid,' he said and in a flash I was awake in my hospital bed, sure that something extraordinary had taken place, and I took some solace in the words of these creatures I assumed my subconscious had invented.

gg

Club foot
Swinging monkey man free
Cock-heavy
and pernicious
With my wings I have flown
to meet you at the crest of the jungle gym
and
prevail

Into the Blue, Blue, Wild Wood

As I lay awake all night I stared out the window, seeing only shadows, cloudy images and the outline of mutant faces, some with disturbing visages, disturbing smiles. The sounds in my head filled the hours and pounded my thoughts like a savage choir, never letting up. I wondered if I was going to get out of here alive, but it seemed increasingly unlikely; I couldn't walk, my voice was a scratchy whisper, I'd lost twenty-five pounds in six weeks, and it didn't escape me that I'd only seen two patients released from intensive care the entire time I'd been conscious. I'd seen another one wheeled out, sheet over face, indicating death, which brought zero comfort or hope.

Now I began to plot my exit. I assumed I was going to die anyway but did not want it to be in this fucking hospital. If I could just get out I would drag myself through town and out into the fields to wait for death.

I struggled to put some clothes on, every move I made completely exhausting me. I could barely put on a pair of socks, it brought on a fight for breath as though I'd run a marathon. My gasping for air woke up one of the other patients, who shot me an evil eye and then rolled over. Years earlier I had woken up in a Swiss hotel room with a collapsed lung, and there had been no mistaking what it was. Now I could feel that same lung was working on maybe thirty per cent and I could barely do a thing for lack of oxygen. It was clear that I wasn't just gonna dance out of here.

The hopelessness and frustration, the utter futility of this now months-long scenario was far beyond anything I'd ever experienced, and I was fully despondent. How many times had I kicked a vicious, painful drug habit? What about the six months I'd been left alone in my house each day while my parents worked, lying on a bed in our living room in a full-body cast after I'd fallen from a bridge, an accident that left me with one leg slightly shorter than the other and a permanent limp? Or how about when my legs were crushed by a tractor while I was working in the pea fields and I'd spent a month on IV blood thinners because of blood clots? Or when

I had lain ten days on a gurney in a Montreal hospital basement hallway on IV antibiotics to save my right arm, swollen twice its normal size with a blood infection from a dirty needle? Or when a doctor had sewn up a gash in my knee only to have it become so infected with gangrene I came one day from having it amputated? What about the time I'd landed in a psych ward in Italy? Flat on my back in four-point restraints, going into heavy withdrawals and nobody understanding my English? And all of those stiflingly boring days and nights in county jail seemed like a trip to the amusement park compared to this.

I didn't care if I ever fucking sang again, as long as I could get out of here. Music was no longer my friend but I left my headphones on round the clock just to keep the outside noise out of my head. How I wished I were still work- ing my old job at Disneyland, or anywhere else in fact. Simple, mindless work, painting, patching, etc. and you were never onstage with anyone paying attention to you.

Finally, I had formed an alliance with a night-time doc who was generous with the sleep and pain meds and he gave me enough to put me to sleep, at least four hours a night.

I closed my eyes and found myself wandering in some woods. In the dark the foliage and sky were deep blue. Exhausted, I lay down on a bed of blue moss and slept like death, hoping I would never wake up again.

Sick as a Dog

Supremely dissatisfied
in physical and psychological pain

how much of my life has been wasted
in this condition?

A large portion
is the answer to that question
You'd think I would have learned how
to avoid this by now
but I always walk straight into it
chin first
like the idiot I am
like the dog I am

Rebuilt

Taken apart
put back together

in many different
shades of blue

The Colossus of Rhodes
destroyed

DEVIL IN A COMA

in an earthquake
was never rebuilt

but I was
            time after time

regardless of the expense

I'm now in your debt
just as I am in so many others'
and I will repay it

when I can
or when I'm forced to

because accepting charity
            makes you weak

and to avoid paying debts
is to ask for trouble
I've learned that much in my time here

It's better to surrender certain battles
and live to fight

another day

The Singer

While I was in the coma and perilously close
to cashing out for good, the doctors went to
my wife asking permission to drill a hole in my
throat and insert some other kind of breathing
apparatus in there. A tracheotomy. They said
it could change the way my voice sounded but
could very well bring me back from the edge
and save me. She informed them that I was a
singer and if they did anything to change the
sound of my voice, that wasn't going to fly. 'He
has a one-of-a-kind voice and to change it in any

way could mean the end of his career and he would rather die than have that happen.' When I heard about this later I was proud of her because she hit the nail on the head: even though my relationship with singing, songwriting, and especially performing, was ambivalent at the best of times, I would rather have been dead than have my voice fucked with in any way. I had spent my life singing myself sick in guitar bands, travelling town to town, country to country, I sang until my head pounded with pain after every performance and the next day I would do it all over again somewhere else. It was all I'd ever had that had possibly done something good for someone, if not myself. Still, when put on the scale, my lifetime of shady actions and misdeeds outweighed anything positive my singing brought to the world by a thousand miles.

MARK LANEGAN

Mile High

Trees a mile high
no foliage just long fingers, arms and
   trunks
white bark, dark blemishes
and silence forever
I came here in my sleep
and felt no human presence
this must have been something from
   memory
or a memory from another life
that I don't remember awake

No matter
a phantom appendage is still aching
long after the limb is gone
like a church or courthouse that I got married
   in
a jail cell or hospital where I stayed awhile

I didn't leave a trace of myself in them either
but they stained me

I wake up in the chair and can see it's still
    raining
Freedom is a multi-edged dagger
at times I was a mindless worker ant
and at others I was one of those with teeth
that stood still and made sure the rest kept
    moving

A lifetime in destruction, tangling,
    untangling, always
travelling with no destination, to finally
    touch down
at this place where there is only one way out

I turn back to the page to obsessively invent
still more damaged and heroic versions of
    myself
before the fire dies out or the well runs dry

constructing imaginary worlds in which no
   opportunity
is missed to undercut the happiness of all
   those
I ever thought did me wrong

wwwwwwwwwwwwwwwwwwwwwwwwww

Thrown Away

As the days, weeks, and months trudged by,
tarantula-slow, I tried to force myself into some
other reality, but the only memories I could
muster were all attached to something I'd rather
forget. The future was an unpromising unknown,
and I could only look to the long-dead past for
comfort, but it seemed as though there was not
one unsullied moment to grab onto. I had spent

my life in the shadows, facilitating my own and others' undoing, taking on nearly any dark task that came my way, every action a means to an end, the end being oblivion. After living on the East Coast for a time, on returning to Los Angeles I had slept for quite a while in a car a friend had given me. Whenever I fell into an intimate relationship it never lasted long. Where was I all night? What was I doing for money? Why was I lying? I never had an honest answer to any of these questions. Nearly every single affair was ended by the woman I was with, not me, and they often left with another man and a knife in my back, which I always had coming. I was a natural at losing, but as soon as one thing ended I was already into something else. Friends kept me afloat with work or a place to stay, often overlooking my questionable behaviour, and I was careful not to burn any of them. They gave me life in a world that would have gladly thrown me away.

Below the Equator

Jungle warfare

the inferno
burned

down to embers

Listening for a phone call
that never rings

Waiting on a letter

that never arrives

¥$£¥$£¥$£¥$£¥$£¥$£¥$$¥$!

Nobody Is Listening

As far back as I could remember, I was
   constantly in trouble with the law
One night
I was taking a piss behind a dumpster
drunk, underage
when the cops came around the corner out of
   nowhere
shined their lights
and said *Hang on a second, bud*
What? I was looking for my wallet, found it,
I said
Who do you think you're kidding, pal?
You're urinating in public
Bullshit, I said
Don't smart me, boy, I'll take you to the
   woodshed
said one of them
I'd like to see you try, I said

Then you're gonna get your wish, kid, the same
    cop said
Subdued in under a minute, I was cuffed,
    hands behind back and
riding in the rear of the cop car down to the
    station, still maintaining my innocence
    and pleading my case that it was a
    misunderstanding
You shut up back there, you little shit!
Now you're done for disorderly conduct AND
    resisting arrest
Disorderly conduct? What the fuck did I do?
I went back there to find my goddamn wallet!
Don't you curse at me, you little fuck! You'll
    be sorry when I've got you in the tanks and
    taking a leak in public IS disorderly conduct,
    you dumbass. I started to protest again
    when the driver suddenly braked hard
    and my face smashed against the Plexiglass
    divider, busting my nose, causing blood to
    shoot out it

Goddamnit, Bob! said the cop riding
   passenger and then they both started
   laughing. As I sat in the back, cuffs so
   tight my circulation was being cut, blood
   soaking my shirt, they drove right past
   the police station and turned back the way
   we came from which alarmed me slightly
   thinking I might be being taken to a REAL
   woodshed somewhere and iced. *Hey guys,
   it's cool I'm a very quiet guy I don't ever talk
   to anybody!*
*Well you sure as hell have talked too much to
   us tonight!*
Special circumstances, I said. *I'll never talk
   about this again!*
Go ahead and talk all you want, kid
he said while pulling up to the same
   dumpster I'd been pissing at earlier,
   getting out, opening the door, uncuffing
   me and shoving me down the alley
Nobody will listen to you anyway.

Desert Goblin

tent pole curiosity

content unknown

half-dog

half-vinegaroon thing

pissed on electric fence

making connection

every god grounded

manual discipline

vimana industry

quicksilver honey of oblivion

lunar circus

revelation antecedent

beyond all belief

Self-Surgery

Age fourteen, having just finished smoking
  some weed behind a parked semi-truck
I was walking up on the elevated ground
where the train tracks used to be
down by the old fairgrounds in my
  hometown
looking at all these clean-cut junior rodeo
  dudes
sitting below on their horses, older, bigger
  than me
and the mouthy friend I was with
Hey you fucking idiots, nice cowboy
  hats!
he yelled out suddenly

Three of them instantly dismounted
and came running up the small hill towards
  us

I straight away tripped my pal backwards
   over my leg, knocking him off his feet and
   ran for
the still-existing trestle that spanned the
   width of
Eighth Avenue and ended where there is now
a Starbucks I believe but used to be
a hamburger joint, my erstwhile companion
   yelled Lanegan, you fucker! And
looking back I saw that my survival tactic
had worked, they were starting to pound on
   the
hapless fool I'd been hanging out with
but right then my foot found empty air
   between the ties
and I went down, gashing my shin and
   ripping my jeans on the
ancient wood
It hurt quite a bit and I limped the rest of
   the distance across, up past 7-Eleven, onto
   the college campus, stole an unlocked ten-

speed and rode to my dad's place out in the
countryside

A couple years later I was drunk one night
sitting on a folding metal chair in my
    filthy bedroom, my father reading a
    book upstairs, never setting foot in the
    basement, which is how I intended it
my thirteen pet rats running around doing
    whatever they wanted
wherever they wanted, my dog Angi
    growling whenever one of them might
    crawl up on her back
or get in her face
my sister out at Ed Nixon's house
and how I idolised him . . .
She knew a rock star when she saw one, I'll
    give her that, the seemingly sophisticated
    charm, charisma and attitude rarely seen
    in our red-neck of the woods, with the
    dominating prowess on the basketball

court to back it up, her boyfriend was my
teenage role model
My mother living in a dismal black-widow-
infested single-wide at 'Desert Aire' a
seedy, rundown trailer park full of older,
bridge-playing gay women down on the
banks of the Columbia river, halfway
through the wastelands to the Hanford
nuclear plant, where she worked, nothing
but
sand dunes as far as the eye could see and
not the inviting kind, either

I was tattooing a crude smiley face on my knee
with a sewing needle, tip wrapped in thread
dipped into a bottle of India ink stolen from
the college bookstore when I paused and
took a look at the long scar on my lower
leg from the train trestle
wipeout a couple calendars earlier. As I felt
and examined it for the first time since

the accident, I could definitely discern

something hard in there under the skin,

big, too

and peering at the semi-translucent scar

tissue with my bedside flashlight I thought

I could see something dark in there as well

I took my folding buck knife out of my

pocket

newly sharpened just the day before

and began to do a bit of self-surgery

I cut a long vertical incision down the

entire length of the scar causing blood to

immediately start pouring onto the cement

floor of my room

I kept cutting, drinking, blasting Hendrix

full volume, this was gonna take a while,

the wound had been deep, scar tissue

shiny but tough

I looked up and saw a line of rats with Angi

in the middle, all standing side by side

greedily lapping up the blood pooled there

as a result of my handiwork. I kept digging
  and finally reached pay dirt, prying out
a four-inch-long thick sliver of prehistoric
  shellacked
railroad tie wood that had been buried in my
  leg for years because
I had never cleaned it out or even looked at it
  before that night
From then on when discussing our plans for
  the future
I'd always tell my shitbag pals I was gonna go
  to med school in the Caribbean
when I got the fuck out of that two-bit town.
  As if.

Favourite Games

Once again I'm working late
forsaking sleep

crawling like a snake

Now it's time to play my favourite game

the one I learned from you

Falling Star

Spring had come and I was still laid up in the sickbed. Besides the bitterness that was flowing out of me due to my circumstances, I was also aware of the global situation, and the knowledge that I would not be allowed to go anywhere even if I were released put me into a mood verging on hopelessness. I had been travelling for over thirty years and the thought of having that taken away struck me as catastrophic. The only thing that had ever kept me engaged was whatever door opened in front of me, and I would always go through it, never knowing what was on the other side. Now I couldn't see a door or any other way out, just a darkness, and who knew what would happen to someone like me who had caught this dread malady? Would I be quarantined indefinitely or locked up in some kind of sanatorium? Sure, they were giving people vaccines now, but I had missed that boat — there wasn't anything to be done if you'd caught it already. It's hard to know where you are when you're trying to read a map by the light of a falling star.

ZZZXXXXZZZXXZXZZZXXZZZZZZZZZZCXXXXXXZZZ

What is it down there?
Throw a stone into the ravine . . .
Release a torn kite into an updraft
and set a newspaper boat adrift
with lit candle cargo
out across stagnant pools

I taste washing-up liquid on my sugar spoon
ashes in my coffee cup
regret in your kiss and
imminent oblivion
in my restless sleep

....,.,....,,,,,,,,,,,,,,

Pray for Me / Conspiracy Theory

I was not religious, nor was my father. My mother was Catholic. Having been raised by fanatic Christian cultists, my father had a particularly virulent strain of anti-religion in him which he passed on to me, and getting either of us to participate in some godly farce was like getting a vampire into a church. As time rolled slowly by and my condition didn't change, however, I began thinking about a paranormal cure, but of course that was just so much wishful bullshit. If there really were a vengeful god I had every expectation of having some excruciating hurt thrown at me. It would have looked at me and seen what I'd done, and no doubt would have made me pay.

I started wondering about this ⸳epidemic on a larger scale and came to the conclusion that there was probably an agenda behind it. Erosion of conventional family and business, implication of one-world government and all that jazz. The best way to take people's freedom is in incremental stages until it's too late to reverse the course of history and a huge global cataclysm was the fastest and easiest way to start that ball rolling. When had my mind begun to turn this way? Oh, right . . . whenever I had done uppers with nothing downtown to balance them out. Under those circumstances these ideas seemed reasonable enough to me. But then again, in only four years fifty per cent of Europe's population died from bubonic plague, two hundred million dead, and in 1918 the Spanish Flu had infected a third of the world's population, wiping out fifty million, so what the fuck did I know? Not a goddamn thing, in fact. At any rate, shit was starting to get very dark in my mind and as I had hours of boredom and nothing much else to think about, these various conspiracies and black thoughts began to invade my head. In Ireland people would not dream of being sold out to globalists by politicians. To me it not only looked possible but probable. Here and everywhere else.

Planned, Executed

I'll be goddamned if this wasn't planned
Too perfect
Too scripted
Too prepared
Too quickly clamped down
Too many dead
Too thought out
Too fucking wrong
And too goddamned planned out
As I may have mentioned before

Alternate Life

While I lay intubated in a coma for three weeks
my mind was having a field day, living it up. I
imagined I was travelling wherever, playing

music, fighting, fucking, etc. Fifteen years earlier I had been in a coma for eight days and then just woke up. No visions or nightmares, just blackness. That was far from the case this time around. The people populating this dream land-scape were a mixture of those I knew from real life, those I vaguely recognised from somewhere, and an entirely new cast of characters my chem-ically sleeping brain invented. In one moment I would be trying to swim a river wild and wide, as dark as it was deep. In another moment I was dangling on the edge of a cavernous quarry, trying to hang on. I was flying on a private jet, participating in my favourite sexual escapades, raising hell, all manner of crazy shit. When I was brought out of this prolonged induced slumber, I was incredulous at what I was being told, it seemed like a joke. The life I had lived during the coma was so vividly real, I had a hard time believing it was not. The fact that I had been out for twenty-one days shook me some, but much of what I had experienced during that time was indelibly stamped on my brain – how could it not be real? As I started going through these bent-backwards recollections I realised something that gave away the truth: I had been barefoot throughout all these adventures. That's when I admitted to myself the real nature of these memories. I would never be without my boots on. In fact, I had even slept with them on for long stretches of my life, in case I had to get out in a hurry.

    Mid-January
    the dogs
    and dregs
    of winter
    I've always had a bad habit
    well, several bad habits
    but one in particular
    is the tendency to mirror my surroundings
    with my mood

turning dark again

courting havoc

and mayhem

fucking shit up as usual

A manager I once had told a girlfriend of
  mine

Lanegan is the Titanic

you'd better get off before he goes down

She didn't listen

and then wished she had

But that was in Los Angeles

years ago

What was my excuse then?

The truth is I could turn brilliant sunlight

dark as the grave

with my deadly powers of perception

I guess it's all in

how you choose to look at things

ttttttttttttttttttttttttttttttttttttttttttttttttttttttttttttttt

The Luck of a Soldier

I was told I was to begin physiotherapy and the next day a porter came in, put me in a wheelchair and took me down to the basement gymnasium. Three doctors watched as I managed to hit every mark taped on the floor using a walker. I was cold and uncomfortable but I also knew that my quickest route out of there was to perform as if I were unimpaired so I concentrated on getting the job done. After one circuit, however, my breathing was so laboured it echoed loudly through the room. This wasn't going to work, getting oxygen was so difficult it was still as bad as it had been when they'd brought me there in the first place. Wheezing, dry coughing, and a deep, echoing sound from down in my chest made it clearly obvious that I was far from well. As a teenager I smoked weed around the clock and developed a loud hacking cough that was so overwhelming I was sometimes asked to leave the classroom due to the disruption it caused. After a harrowing bad acid trip I was unable to smoke weed anymore without bringing on a flashback, my saviour having viciously turned on me, and when I quit I would for weeks cough pure black mucus out of my lungs which got lighter in colour until after six months it was a dull grey. As I was always in trouble with the law, my probation officer suggested I join the National Guard and that sounded reasonable to me. I thought it would get me out of town and trouble. At age fifteen I had to get my father's OK, and he signed the forms though against his wishes and he told me so. He had been in the army himself and got out just before the Vietnam War, his experience an apparently unhappy one. As I sat down to take the four-hour written test, I quickly concluded that I knew shit about shit. Every single question was so far beyond my comprehension that I left page after page totally blank. Once I was done, I had my father rescind his approval and with that, the luck of a soldier had once again turned, and I continued to careen like a demented pinball off anything and anyone in my way, piling up a small mountain of sorrow, calamity, sadness and trauma.

!!!

The Darkest Part

At times I've struggled to love life
and when a huge flock of blackbirds
roll across the sky
I wish I could go with them

When a woman gives herself to me
and all my loneliness
it's more than I deserve

DEVIL IN A COMA

When mist hangs on the water
and I have learned another lesson hard
it's straight to the darkest part of me
and a lesson is hard to take
when it's the painful kind
but I will take it every time

and the suffering that I endure
and all the pain that I have caused
will someday be the sorry end of me
so I apologise now

and though I have often failed
and I will again
God knows the better part of me

::,,,,,,,4::::::::::::::::::::::::::::
....

MARK LANEGAN

Outside Myself

It was like I was standing outside myself

I know that feeling

looking at myself from a distance

like I were there but not really

as though it were someone else doing it
not me

I've experienced these phenomena
multiple times
and problems of perception
can drive some people to distress

Not me, though
In a way, they've saved me

because even if I've paid a price at times
for some of my baser behaviours
mostly it was like I was
never even there to begin with

grey sky

grey
    grey sky
I left you behind full-time
        twenty-odd years ago
I moved to the desert to escape the rain
or so I said, but it was really to escape myself
didn't work, obviously
the circular nature of life
has never escaped *me* though
        just like I said I'd never
cook again, and then learned to grudgingly
  enjoy it as an

inexpensive form of therapy, to. clear. my.

   aching. head.

here I am back in the gloom

and

the doom

doing interviews on zoom

from my cold, rainy island kingdom

     in exile

…..?...??????????????????????????

Going Bad

As April turned to May I found myself sliding
into what felt like black-mood clinical depression and I was on the precipice of losing a fight
against it. I had to leave the hospital and that was

the only thing I thought about all day. Everyone who interacted with me, porters, nurses and doctors, all knew I was obsessed with getting out and all of them used any opportunity to talk me into staying. My mind was starting to go bad again, I began going over and doubting every decision that had brought me here. Hellhounds at my back in Los Angeles, I had rashly put my house up for sale, sold it in less than three weeks and bought a plane ticket to Ireland before the property was even sold (Ireland being the only country that was allowing United States citizens in at the time). My shaky plan was to land in Dublin, quarantine for a couple of weeks and then move on to Portugal, my preferred destination. My pal Donal Logue owned a home in County Kerry that was sitting empty at the time and when he offered it to me I was grateful. Once I had seen the physical beauty of the place and quickly made some friends I decided fuck it, I'll stay here. After all, it was the place where my oldest known ancestors had come from and I had always enjoyed great audiences whenever I played here. The majestic mountains, lakes and forests called me and I listened.

After twenty-three years in Southern California it took a slight adjustment to get used to a cold, wet winter again, but that was nothing, I felt like I had finally made it home. I set up my recording gear and put down a bunch of demos for a future record. Then, with the encouragement of my friend Wesley Eisold, I started obsessively writing poetry. When I had at least three books of poems done I started drawing with charcoal and oil paint on canvas, something I'd never done before, and soon the house was packed with my primitive artwork.

I had been careful to keep to myself when out in public – the last thing I wanted was to catch some shitty virus and die – but when a journalist from Belfast contacted me to do an interview and photo session, I agreed. The day after he had

been at my house he called to tell me he had tested positive for the COVID-19 virus and he was
sorry. Not knowing if I'd infected him or him
me, I honestly thought OK, no need to panic, I'm
sure if I have it I'll be one of those who just floats
through it as if they have a common cold. But
instead I was one of those who got flattened by
a steamroller. It came on extremely fast and hit
me like a freight train. Within three days of him
calling, I was coming apart at the seams. Deaf,
unable to breathe, unable to walk, and on my
way to the most desperate holiday of my life.

The Back Lot

Goodbye old city
You were good to me
until you were not
Goodbye speed freaks

and dope fiends

So long dealers and gangbangers

strippers, escorts

addicts, roadies and thieves

I'm gonna miss you all

you gotta believe that

because my world is going to be a sadder gig

without you in it

I'm trying to picture how that looks

and I can't quite yet

I guess I'm gonna learn how

but it won't ever be easy

because I've been

plagued with dyslexia all of my life

and I always fall asleep in class

and never do my studies

because I'm

always lost in dreaming

44444...

............445555,,,,,,,,,,,,,,,,,(((((,,,,,,:,,,,,(((((;;;;;;;(((

....

???

.

Chemical Protection

As far as I know
the only times I've had multiple personalities
were when I was in an alcohol-
induced blackout
then I was definitely another animal
just tiny visual flashes or no memory at all
of what I said or did

That can be somewhat off-putting
the days and weeks following a bender

especially if the other thing you became

had a propensity towards violence, crime

and erratic behaviour

in the sleeping state

like my shadow-self did

I recall my first court-ordered 12-step
      meeting at age fourteen, 1978

The guy running the show, a burly, surly-
      looking old dude said, 'I woke up in a jail
      cell in 1957 and they told me I'd killed a
      man. Then I spent the next eighteen and
      a half years in the penitentiary without
      any memory of having done it.' And
      afterwards my buddy who I'd bribed into
      giving me a ride and attending it with me
      said, 'Goddamn Lanegan I swear if you
      keep drinking, that's gonna happen to
      you.' Luckily it didn't, but everyone who
      was friends with me at that time knew at a
      certain point my brain might shut off and
      my body would keep going. For miles, in

fact. And around the age of fifteen I said
to myself, man, you're gonna have to quit
drinking someday, but thank God you'll
always have weed. And that shines a small
ray of light on my mindset most of my life.
I've never enjoyed being fully present,
a muted reality has been the landscape
I've preferred and mainly inhabited
forever. Sure, feeling is good, but not too
much, and if someone is able to get away
with suffering devastating loss, massive
regret, heartache, physical agony, mental
instability, isolation, humiliation, abuse,
incarceration, depression, tragedy, etc.,
with a blanket of chemical protection, then
who can say it's wrong?
Yes, I've run myself ragged at times and put
myself through the mill but when someone
poses the question: How did he survive?, it
might be that they are not operating with
the full spectrum of the circumstances.

Whatever

I spilled gin all down my shirt
I took a piss and missed the bowl
I watched Kurosawa all day long
and wept all night like a weak fuck
crawling the carpet
I was a viper, too
I could have poisoned the entire
municipal
water supply with my venom
like I poisoned myself
whatever came my way, I did
a garbage can, an incinerator, a lowest-rent
Bill Burroughs
or so I might have thought
but chemicals don't = talent
As is the case with so many
great pretenders . . .
I've been

A. Quick with the cowardly disappearing
act
   B. Constantly throwing red on white walls
C. Always crying those lame crocodile tears
   D. Caught more than once rifling through
somebody's coffin

....
!!

OOOOOOOOOOOOOOOOOOOOOOOOOOOOOOOOOOOO

???????!!???????????

Do You Remember Me? / Say Something New

As my diseased body continued to lie on a hospital bed, my diseased mind was continuing to devour itself. I had never come up against anything I couldn't beat or escape before and the coronavirus turned out to be the mythical beast that had my number, teaching me beyond all doubt that you can't outrun what you can't see. My patience and strength were totally gone, and though I kept waiting for some improvement in my condition, it was not forthcoming; in fact many days I felt as though I were still getting worse. Toughness, tenacity, balls, fire, audacity and a rock-solid getaway plan had always been my strengths in any battle, but they were not going to serve me here, far from it. I may as well have been a caterpillar fighting a crow . . . toothless. I was well used to having my fortunes turn on a dime and the bottom dropping out, but I was also used to having a plan B, C, D, etc. to fall back on. This thing refused to let me go, and for the first time ever I sensed I were completely helpless, an unfamiliar state that not only stoked a fiercely confused rage but also a total rethink of everything I had imagined to be true. Could it really be possible that after whistling through the graveyard for all these years I was finally going to be put down? Like this?? No fucking way. Every time these questions ran through my head my immediate response was *I'll be damned if I go out like this, no fucking way*. Plane crash, auto crash, gunfire, murder . . . when I imagined my death these had always looked like the most likely candidates, and it made me particularly angry that my life could end like this, lying in a goddamned bed, denied a battlefield.

As I looked around the room it was impossible to gauge my condition based on the other patients. Everyone was at least twenty years my senior and honestly, none of them seemed very sick to me, just very, very old. A friendly night-time doctor from South Africa had looked me up on the internet and was now an enthusiastic fan of my singing. One night he dropped by to share with me his ideas on how to achieve future success once I was released. If I were to follow his plan, I could easily pay off not only my huge medical bill, but also make a million bucks on top of it. I had heard similar musings many times before from other well-wishing souls but what I really needed was for someone to say something new, because at this stage of the game it seemed to me exceedingly doubtful that I was going to survive this ordeal, much less ever sing again, destined to fade into nothingness, a tiny stain on history, forgotten already and any notion to the contrary had to be some fucked-up magical thinking.

Case Study

Go ahead and do as I've done

                        crawl like a slug

eat garbage   break yourself in
   two

              sleep with trash

will yourself into oblivion

             crack yourself into the
   netherworld

drink yourself to death

         reduce yourself to nothing

become a rabid animal

        camp out next to the freeway in the
   rain

carry balloons in your mouth

          swallow them if need be

search through your shit to find them again

   draw up water into a rig off the hood of a
   car

MARK LANEGAN

hide behind a dumpster
                    cook it up
in the torn-off bottom of an aluminium can
and shoot
                         disappear before you are
    found
get out before they catch you
          chew off a limb if you are trapped
blast out the windows with a gun
                              point it at your
    associates
and yourself
              and nearly pull the trigger again
be spit on
                                   discounted
disregarded
                   laughed at
                   written off
given up for dead
                     and then fuck shit up by
    living

to tell the tale of your destruction

        and who you encountered

on the way to the killing floor

          inhabit a thousand dive

  rooms

a hundred jail cells

        fifty rehab beds

a dozen psych wards

       walk the streets all night, every

  night

scream at yourself like a dictator

    comport yourself like the freak you are

cut loose from any friends

                        or

  family

dance into the grave

        and out again

sing like a wounded grizzly bear

        or a disinterred

  mummy

and fuck yourself to the very gates of Hades

and back out

There. How'd that feel?

Some people experience freedom
in being completely unhinged
and lost out on the flip-side of polite society

but it takes some balls

a battleship full of psychic willpower
or flat-out insanity
along with a shitload of stamina
and a grip of self-hatred

but no brains at all
to find it

Good luck with that

Part of the Equation

Still suffering from brutal insomnia, not able to shut my head off, painful memories of my youth and adulthood and the mental corrosion of my present situation not letting me go, the regrets, mistakes and the overwhelming sadness of a wasted life that looked like it could very likely be over at any time, when I felt like I had so much more I needed to put right. I was now being weaned from sleep and pain meds, something that cast me into an even darker mood than I had been in previously. As I lay awake night in, night out my musings were difficult to get a handle on. What would my chances of survival be had I caught this thing in Los Angeles or somewhere else, a place with a larger population and more medical facilities? I came to the conclusion that my chances were actually better here. My wife had told me that the entire time I had been in the coma and on kidney dialysis, I had been the only patient in a large empty room, and knowing that I was receiving such specialised treatment gave me a modicum of mental relief. And I was grateful for Shelley's vigilance. I'd been told that she had sat there bedside for several hours a day, keeping a lonely watch. But it took less than a second for my perspective to flip and see things from the other side, and a sunny day was suddenly midnight black. As wildly unhinged as I had lived, I was always aware of the looming spectre of death, most of my closest friends already dead for years. I had always known I was operating on borrowed time. My condition had not changed for quite some time, still not able to walk, my voice just a ghostly whisper, daily battles with staff over my continued refusal to give blood or eat, and I was sure I was finally close to going permanently lights out. But that was only part of the equation. The other part was my stubborn refusal to let go of this current dark

reality, no matter how bleak, painful or hopeless
that might look.

Mostly Dead

They're almost all gone now
my old gang
I'm in my fifties
but most of them died in their twenties
or early thirties at best
It's been a long, lonesome couple of decades
out here in the wilderness alone
I treasure laughter when it comes and
lean towards some new alliances
as well as the few that are left behind
like me
but there's not many around these days
This is the price I have paid for stubbornness
and recalcitrance

amongst many other shortcomings
I have never really known
how to give up the ghost

....b.........................

Zero Charm

With a dead-eyed vacancy I had come up out
of the endless, deserted, wind-whipped fields of
eastern Washington state, between the Cascade
mountains to the west and desert to the east. A
pugilistic know-nothing nobody, midnight train
whistle and pockets full of rocks in case of an
attack by dogs while walking the long country
roads to my house at night, a common occurrence. I did not make friends easily and I was
constantly fighting with anyone at all, never

backing down even if it meant getting my ass kicked, which it often did. I spent my solitary youth looking for any chance to steal anything that presented itself, living to get loaded, obsessively taking my classmates' money with gambling devices I had spent hours modifying to make sure no one would win but me. One of my first girlfriends said, 'I really want to like you, but it's fucking impossible,' and that statement set the stage for countless relationships going forward. I didn't know how to ride easy and I had no interest in learning how. To do that was contrary to everything I believed, to ride easy was to set yourself up to get fucked, and not in a pleasurable way, either. If you were not a soldier on the wall you were an abject defeatist, and in my book there was no in between. The dysfunctional home life I enjoyed made me place my reliance strictly on myself and nobody else, I trusted no one and no one should have trusted me either; I was only in it for yours truly and stood directly in the centre of the world, the only wolf in the pack. I got by through imitation, acting as human as possible, but there was an exceptionally ugly and devious animal just below the surface and it was quick to strike whenever it felt threatened.

Sledgehammer

I took a sledgehammer to a car
for charity
It cost five hundred and forty-eight days
a year with good behaviour
Drove and drove and drove
with no destination
Coach Sweeney wanted me to be a lineman
I had other plans
You're not a quarterback, never gonna be a
quarterback, he yelled once

and then suddenly I was . . .

long enough to throw a ton of interceptions

get a few concussions and grow to hate the
   sport of American football

My teammates already hated me

After taking a vicious hit to the head

I puked in the fireplace after a game

My old man put down his newspaper and said

What the hell?

My bell got rung hard so many times

and I always had it coming

I'd have shit-talked the president, or Jesus

My default state of being

no fucks given. To a grievous fault

it's amazing I got out alive

but of course there's no way on earth

it's gonna last forever

/// //////////////////////

###############################

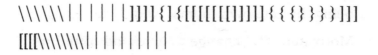

In the Arms of an Overpowering Malaise

I had reached a turning point. There was no possible way I could stay in the hospital any longer, and even though I was still not able to walk unaided, I was leaving. My first order of business was talking my wife into my plan, which wasn't easy since she knew she would basically become my caregiver until I was well. After stressing the point that I was fine, or at least I soon would be, she finally agreed, and then I had to have similar conversations with several doctors and nurses. Francie agreed with me, he could see that I was gripped by an over-whelming malaise, and thought, as I did, that being in my own home would do me good. Motivated for change, my mood lifted as I anticipated getting out. I overlooked the difficulty of just getting from a wheelchair into the taxi, and again from car to my couch, but once it was done, I sat there fighting for air again. I instantly started to question my decision, and thought about the multitude of times and ways I had fucked myself in the past by not listening to the opinions of those who knew so much more than me. Had I set myself up for my final undoing? Should I have stayed? The scorpion had become drunk on his own venom as usual and when that commonly occurred I was only able to see things from one perspective, my own.

Bleeding Out

Slice through the pulsating jugular

bleed me out

prop up my cadaver

dress it in a black suit

take its photo

and print up a new wanted

   poster

'captured' this one says

but it should really say 'murdered'

I've been caught again

the animal put down

I've heard it said that a person has lived

   infinite lifetimes

I have lived a thousand

wrapped up in this one here

The loop repeats, over and over

one ends, another begins
so fast it could turn your stomach

the wretched carousel
revolving ever faster
until it throws you off
onto the muddy ground
surrounding the ride
and lining the floor
of the itinerant carnival midway

Straight Razor Sharp

For the first few days I was home, I could still
not walk normally, sleep for any decent stretch,
eat without the food making me sick, or find any
real joy in anything even though I had managed
to mostly throw off the shroud I wore in the
hospital. After a while I started dragging myself

upstairs by sitting on the steps and pulling myself up backwards with my hands. Eventually I was walking without a walker.

Ten weeks in and I was still in a good amount of pain though, my lungs aching, chest sore, leg discomfort keeping me awake at night. This illness also seemed to unlock something in my subconscious, and I was dreaming more than I had ever remembered doing before. Vivid imaginings that seemed to mainly echo my real life experiences the first ten years or so I had spent in Los Angeles: driving all night like a maniac, hauling ass in my piss-yellow Buick from San Diego to Bakersfield, Venice to Joshua Tree and back again. As I tried to fall asleep at night the previous night's imaginings would come back and I would start mind-travelling again.

The days still crept by like a snail, and I sometimes thought that whatever damage I may have suffered from Covid might be permanent; just as I had experienced while in hospital, any noticeable change in my physical condition was so incremental as to feel intangible. I waited day in, day out for that to turn, trying my damnedest to stay calm and find some patience, but patience was far from being a strong suit of mine. I faced a daily war between my hopeful perception and what felt like an unchanging and still-dark-as-fuck reality, made more poignant by the baseline fact that no one could really give me any truthful information about a person's future once they had caught the virus and survived. Was it going to come back at some point and finish the job of rubbing me out? Was I going to carry residuals from it for the rest of my days? What about mobility? Was I ever going to get back to where I was before this shit began? How fucked was I, really?

I would lie awake all night, fall asleep in daylight, and wake up in the late afternoons while sundown was already coming on and wish to God I had not woken up at all. More and more

when I did sleep, though, my mind played a
straight razor-sharp death dream on an endless
loop.

   this vacant tomb

calls out

come, I'm waiting for you!

a she-wolf rips your skin

the melancholy buries you alive

a heretic recuses

tuberculosis, cotton fever and

   plague

the big top folds up and leaves

the elephant sleeps

the dead planets turn and turn

   and turn

and turn

turning you sapphire

making you untouchable

making you golden

folding you into ether

making you

stardust

wwwwwwwwwwwwwwwwwwwwwwwwww

Music of Silence

My interest in music was non-existent. I never put on a record or picked up a guitar or sat
at the keyboard and didn't care if I ever did a
gain. Years earlier I had experienced a similar
falling-out with music – also on the heels of a
coma – but where that had disturbed me somewhat, and made me worry about how I was going
to get by, this time I didn't think twice. I already
had enough weight on my mind without adding
to the stress and strain. Music would come back

to me or it wouldn't, and I was going to live with that, either way. But first I had to learn how to walk and talk again, because my feet no longer knew where they were going, and my voice had forgotten how to sound.

Some healthcare workers came to my house to do physical therapy with me and were enthusiastic as to my progress in the two weeks I had been out. They said they had expected to need specialised equipment just to get me around the house and were surprised that I was now walking up and down the stairs, no walker, and even though I was still ultra-shaky, I could see the progress and was determined to put this brutal affair behind me, even though nobody had any idea how long a recovery from this goddamn thing would take, simply because nobody knew jack shit about this virus. As the physical therapy workers were leaving, one of the women asked if I had any more questions for them. All of us laughed because any questions were unanswerable, everyone was in uncharted waters, everything blind speculation. After being home for a while, I started to regain a bit of energy, enough to start responding to the huge pile of emails and texts from friends and family; I would fire off a few each day. My most staunch supporters were those I had loved forever and who had always been there for me no matter how badly I had behaved, how stupidly I had acted, or how many times I put them through the emotional wringer by tightrope walking so far above where I had any right to, and diving way past my depth on an endless search for what I was never going to find.

Black Moon Red Sun

Purple moss dangling, alive, reaching
Fog rolls across

ancient palms

cleaning windows

scaling volcanic mansions

reaching a forgiving crest

Shadows dissolved

diseased countenance

fires extinguished

rope harnessed

heavy serge military coat

propane reignited

handgun stolen

dry firing rough trade

asphalt and addiction

lungs hacking black

from nuclear sickness

shackled at neck

light sensitive

and blindness

I'm in the back of a car

dreaming *aurora borealis*

Only Part-Way Back

After being home for a couple of weeks, still in a black mood due to the slow progress of my physical recovery routine, and mainly stranded inside due to the icy, windy weather and Covid restrictions, I was rummaging around in my travel bag to find a razor to shave off the huge, ridiculous beard I had grown, when I came across a lone painkiller. I quickly chewed it up and swallowed it. My immune system was still so compromised I went into a severe coughing fit, gasping for breath but not able to breathe, and I passed out. I came to back in the hospital again, Francie himself wheeling me through the lower floors of the institution to the X-ray and CT scan rooms to see what kind of damage I had done now. My wife had been forced to call an ambulance once again and she was deeply unhappy with my stubborn, stupid, thoughtless conduct. I could sense her turning to stone, a common reaction I'd seen before. But whenever I looked back, I could rarely ever feel I'd done wrong, could never remember what I'd done or the reason why. But now, after everything, I was back where I'd tried so hard to escape from, and it was due to my own actions. I had foolishly left too early, against all advice.

Drifting in and out of consciousness I was half-aware that they were taking the opportunity to search for veins, and felt jab after jab in my arms as they failed to hit one. Coming to for a minute a few hours into the afternoon, I found that they had put a stent line into my knee and that was working for them, much to my relief. As I was being brought from place to place for more tests, not enough energy to lift my chin off my chest, I felt a slight twinge of regret whenever I rolled past one of the doctors or nurses who had tried so hard to talk me into staying a couple of weeks prior. Mainly I tried to ignore such feelings and continued to confidently act as if it didn't bother me, but when a particularly attractive doctor who had spent quite a while trying to convince me to stay earlier greeted me, I couldn't help but feel a momentary ache of shame. Shame for putting myself so quickly back into this same situation I had fought so vehemently to escape, with such boringly predictable tactlessness and such unseemly idiocy. Goddamn it ... I was sure after a lifetime of doing as I pleased no matter the cost, I was too far gone to ever stop behaving in these impetuous, often deadly, ways, and knew from painful experience in what passed for my heart that each and every time I walked out into the dark, I only ever came part of the way back.

I quickly shook it off and told myself I didn't care if I was right or wrong. And that had always been my problem. One of my many, many problems.

Vicious

Sickening waves
gathering speed
slamming down
dragged back out to sea

My body is who I am
battered, bruised, beaten
and soulless

Violent instinct
ridiculous dreams
harsh reality

I suppose I owe you a thanks
You could have killed me
but you didn't
but I won't let my guard down again
you can count on that

Re-entry is a motherfucker
but tenacity is a virtue in my book
if you have the strength for it
and I do

You said you've known guys like me before
but in that notion you've made a slight
    miscalculation
What you thought was the end
is only just now beginning

/// /////////////////////
/////////////////
###
#####

//////////:·····//////////:·;·;;;//////////:·····//////////:·····-
/////:·····//

Half Full / Brutality of Ageing

Back in the hospital due to pneumonia in my lungs and infection in my blood, as well as what I would characterise as a dubious overdose, were anyone asking my opinion, which, of course, nobody was.

I landed on the same ward where I'd recently spent months fighting to survive a murderous strain of coronavirus. I found that the geriatric company I was keeping now was even older than those I had been in with previously. Directly across from me was an angry old woman who I had seen try to knock a food tray out of a porter's hands, as well as yell some indistinguishable words over and over at the same young girl. This woman spent hours singing a loud, unmelodious song to her moth-eaten teddy bear, having endless conversations with the same stuffed toy, in a high-pitched voice not one word of which could I understand. The man on the other side of her talked loudly and constantly in his sleep, yelling, 'Jesus Christ!' and 'My God!' The continual dismal shrieking of these people and the wailing, moaning and crying of the others set me on edge and I struggled to keep from detonating.

When I was a teenager my Welsh maternal grandmother, an older and unbelievably more monstrous version of my mother, had been put into an elderly care facility in my hometown in a vegetative state. I was forced to accompany my mother as she went through the charade of visiting her mother's nearly lifeless body from time to time, and on one occasion as I walked down the hallway another resident in a wheelchair grabbed my arm and wouldn't let go. After a second I realised this woman was an older friend of my mother's, one of her bridge-playing partners who had always been very nice to me, who had suffered a devastating stroke a few years prior. As I stood there in her grip she looked up at me with the saddest, most desperate gaze I'd ever seen, and in that moment I understood that she recognised me and wanted help. I gently pulled her off me with my free hand, and quickly walked outside and stood in the parking lot. As hard as I tried I couldn't stop myself from crying, the ever-present wind blowing my tears straight back across my face. The harsh injustice of ageing and the helplessness of infirmity was more than I could take. I swore I would die before I ended up like that. When my mother came out to the car and saw my red eyes she impatiently demanded, 'What the hell's wrong with you?'

After more than a year in a coma my grandmother suddenly came to and went on to live for several more years, some of them in our house, making my life even more hellish with her as the other half of my mother's vicious tag team.

Now, in the hospital, I found myself having

these infuriating flashbacks, the youngest in-
mate of that same kind of old folks' prison. I had
failed in my lifelong quest to go out before ending up here, naturally thinking I had years ahead
of me before facing such a situation. At least I
could get myself to the toilet, thank God. All of
these unfortunate old souls had to get their shit-
filled diapers changed, sometimes twice daily,
and every time the workers came round to fulfil
this unpleasant task, the patients put up a fight.
Lots of yelling, cursing and protesting. I felt bad
for these people, and hated being witness to this
indignity they suffered. After living lifetimes of
mobility and self-sufficiency, being reduced to
the humiliation of this routine. Their fierce pride
would have them continue wearing a dirty pad
rather than let a stranger wipe their ass.

During this second stay I started to feel somewhat physically better, able to walk unaided and
sleeping better than before, the cup feeling half
full for once. I couldn't tell if this was actually

some kind of recovery from the virus or just a small lucky streak, but whatever, I was glad to be feeling partially normal for the first time in forever. Of course, this made my urge to leave kick in with even more intensity than before.

///

A friend once told me
it's better to get old than not
considering the alternative
but I am of the Pete Townshend school of
    thought
I hope I die before I get old

///

Delusional

Here in mostly rural Ireland, I found myself looking out the same hospital window I had when I'd first come out of a coma months earlier. The view from my bed brought back memories of my delusional dreaming as I had drifted in and out of consciousness, sure that I were someplace I was not, travelling thousands of miles a day, probably talking shit to whoever I encountered, and wanting to leave, no matter where I really was. It seemed as though the symptoms and pain of the Covid pneumonia that had been beating my ass down so intently had abated – my breathing came slightly easier, and there was less aching, soreness and discomfort in my lungs and upper body afflicting me now. Since my life wasn't deemed to be in immediate danger anymore, my wife was no longer allowed to come and go as she had when the staff here had thought I was on the verge of dying, but luckily Francie lived just five minutes from the hospital and would come by to wheel me out for a smoke now and then.

#%%%#%%%#%^#%^%^^%^^#%#^%

Tarotplane

Split the deck
somebody suspicious
foraging

around covert
operative

Seven of Wands
Queen of
Cups

Seven of Swords
collective
reading ascension

process transformation
light and
dark

oil the
machine
and manifest
upwards

Self-Inflicted

On a Friday afternoon the doctor had told me he
was going to take a look at my lung X-rays and
probably let me go the next day. On Saturday,

however, I saw not one doctor all day long and found out there would be none coming by until Monday. This made me silently furious. Yes, I had possibly nearly died again, but that was days ago. Now I felt better than I had this entire time and there was no way I was staying here until Monday. I was going to try and get a script for the antibiotics they were giving me for my lungs and then I was getting the fuck out. I was particularly unhappy that I was back in here due to my own fucked-up decision-making, but here I was on the edge of repeating the exact same mistake again. I was well aware that no one gave a damn about what I would like to see happen, they were just going to toe the company line. After harassing anybody who walked by with requests to see a doctor, I was finally granted a meeting with one. She listened to my lungs for half a second and said, 'I can't let you go.'

At this I sat up and said, 'Well, I'm going anyway,' and asked what was happening here

DEVIL IN A COMA

that I couldn't do at home. Yesterday I had not seen a physician all day, just lay in bed, endlessly waiting for the time to pass. I was more than able to do this same thing at my own house, and emphatically told her so. Another hour or so crawled by, she then reappeared with a waiver form that I hastily scribbled on and was released against advice once again, but not before being warned that my blood showed levels of infection and I had better see a GP in no less than two weeks.

Impossible Odds

Story of my life

My sex history book in shreds

like a naked body

thrown into the thorny windmill
of an angry, inconsolable
rose garden

An unforgiving read

but at least I can say
I've never gone to bed
with any monsters

I only woke up with a few dozen or so

############################

\\\\\\|||||||]]]}{}{[[[[[[[]]]]}{{}}}]]][[[[\\\\\\\\|||||||||

And the Band Played On

Meanwhile, people were dying by the hundreds daily in India where the pandemic was in full-on fucked-up swing. Most Western countries were working overtime to try to get people vaccinated but that was not the case everywhere. Bodies of the Covid dead were being tossed into the Ganges river and unfortunate multitudes were literally expiring in the streets, fighting for breath, no room for the dying in the hospitals and nothing to be done about it. Only the wealthiest citizens could afford to lock themselves up in their homes, stocked up on food, so as to never have to come into contact with the millions in the streets, and by doing so escape this hideous plague.

As I read the accounts of these horrors I recognised once again how lucky I had been to be treated in Ireland, which was one of the first places to get hit hard and seemed to have a pretty good playbook on how to keep people alive by the time I landed in the hands of the medical professionals here. The doctors and nurses all ultra-kind and concerned, working hard around the clock to see to the patients' comfort and well-being. I felt a cutting, raw chagrin when I thought about my obvious, self-centred juvenile impatience, bordering on rudeness at times, rarely making things easy on these selfless workers who were doing their best just to see me live, to help me survive this thing. I wanted to get my head screwed on right and start exhibiting some heavily owed gratitude towards these people, but I was not equipped for such nuances and could not bear to hide my unhappiness. This continued stay, now well over three months, was brutalising my mind.

Almost as soon as my course of antibiotics was finished, it became difficult to breathe again, my lungs and back wracked in pain with every breath I fought to take. When I went to my meeting with the GP he took a quick listen to my lungs and said, 'You need to go back to the hospital immediately or you're going to die.'

ꞓꞓꞓꞓꞓꞓꞓꞓꞓꞓꞓꞓꞓꞓꞓꞓꞓꞓꞓꞓꞓ

The lake
frozen over, white
and dull grey, icy-blue hues

A squadron went off the radar
and disappeared nearby
in rough terrain

This is God's country, or so it is said
but it's also death's country
don't forget that

ZZ

The Last Go-Round

Shocked stupid by the doctor's adamant, candid insistence regarding my upcoming death, I still could not stand the thought of returning a third time to the Kerry hospital, especially after I had left twice already against all advice. Despite the care shown to me by everyone there, my fucked-up pride would not allow it. The next day my close friend Tony O'Flaherty, a talented local music producer/engineer who I often hung out and recorded with, drove me to the university hospital in Cork, a much larger city and facility. I had actually recorded a song for someone with Tony in his studio later in the same day I had caught the virus – he tested negative a day later, much to my relief. It would have been tough to live with had I infected him or his family. Now we rode mainly in silence, masks over our faces, on the old two-lane road from Killarney down to Cork. Passing closed-up pubs, churches and chip shops, wind blowing the long green grass and leaves on the trees like waves on the ocean, flocks of sheep and herds of cattle lounging in the fields. We finally arrived at three p.m., and as I got out of the car, my wife looked into my eyes and, thinking it might be the last time she'd see me, said, 'Baby, I love you.' I walked away towards the hospital doors.

I was quickly admitted at the emergency entrance, and then waited for six long, frustrating hours before being seen by a woman who (unsurprisingly) struggled to find a vein. She managed to get one eventually, the deep red-black blood oozing out syrup-slow, her saying, 'C'mon! Don't stop!' until her syringe was totally full. I was then left sitting in the cement-stiff chair for another three hours before I was called into the back to see a doctor. After listening to my lungs and heart he ordered yet one more CT scan and round of X-rays which all came back healthy, but he was worried I may have had a blood clot. After being told not to move in case I shook a clot loose, I lay my six-foot-two-inch frame on a thin, rock-hard five-foot-long cot in the brightly lit room until morning when I was to see a different physician for more tests.

A few hours later another doctor and a couple of interns came by. He asked me what had brought me here. When I told him what the GP had said he laughed and shook his head.

'Well, that was a bit dramatic ... and you decided to wait another day before coming in? The tests show me that your blood, lungs and kidneys are healthy and all your symptoms are common post-Covid.'

With that he prescribed some more antibiotics, steroids, an inhaler and some blood thinners and after making an appointment to be seen at the clinic there in a month, the ghost revived once more, I walked out into the light drizzling rain and grey morning skies, for the first time with the blessing of the doctors. The ravages of the virus would go on to take a very long time to heal, but I got into a cab, cautiously optimistic that I might finally be on my way towards something resembling freedom. Freedom being relative, of course.

@@@@@@@@@@@@@@@@@@@@@@@@@@

The Softer Landing

Let me fall
but let me rise
don't let heaven or hell
and me collide

to be a horse

to be a train

I wouldn't have the heart

next to the tracks

you see a ghost

wearing a sling

the mockingbird

you hear it weeping

until all is done

and down to dust

when kingdom comes

you will be singing

a song of hope

a song of love

caught in your throat

so never ending

} {} {} {}} #}}}}}}} {{{{## {{{}} {} {}}
{}} {}} ###} {}} {}}}
88888888888888888888888888888888

Acknowledgements

Shelley Brien

Amy Lee

Wesley Eisold

Lee Brackstone

Richard Machin

Ben Schafer

Gus Brandt

Mishka Shubaly

Roberto Bentivegna

Donal Logue

Joe Cardamone

Aoife Woodlock

Paolo Bicchieri

Francie Breen

143

ACKNOWLEDGEMENTS

Tony O' Flaherty

Trina Lanegan

David Coppin-Lanegan

Rosie Pearce

Ellie Freedman

White Rabbit Books

Hachette Books

Heavenly Recordings

Alessio Natalizia

Gerard Johnson

Karl O' Connor

Rob Marshall

Sietse van Gorkom

Greg Dulli

Jeff Barrett

Leila Moss

Robert Chandler

Aidan O'Connell

Michael Logue

Jimi Shields

Ava Stroud

ACKNOWLEDGEMENTS

Teo Bicchieri

Toby Butler

Duke Garwood

Clay Decker

Christophe Claeys

Warren Ellis

Becky Muter

Dylan Carlson

Laurie Davis

Talulah James

Romi Pearl

Martyn LeNoble

Sonny Garwood Mackey

James Dean Bradfield

Dede Alva

Scott Brien

Emily Mackey

Dean Duzenski

Michael 'Curly' Jobson

Roy Van Akkeren

Christian Huwiler

ACKNOWLEDGEMENTS

Aldo Struyf

Aeneas Healy

Frederic Lyenn Jacques

Jeff Fielder

Alain Johannes

Randall Jamail

The staff of Kerry hospital, Tralee, Ireland